AF382622

STRENGTHEN YOUR LINKEDIN PROFILE

The ideal tool for networking and job searching

Written by Maïlys Charlier
Translated by Rebecca Neal

Coaching 50MINUTES.com

LINKEDIN: A VITAL TOOL FOR PROFESSIONAL RELATIONSHIPS

- **Problem:** how can you use LinkedIn to expand your circle of professional contacts?
- **Uses:** using LinkedIn will enable you to network effectively and increase your visibility on the job market.
- **Professional context:** networking, job search, customer prospecting, recruitment, communication, personal branding.
- **FAQs:**
  - Should LinkedIn be used to complement other social networks?
  - Should I publish personal information on LinkedIn?
  - Should I list all my professional experience on my profile?
  - Should I make my LinkedIn profile public?
  - Is there a difference between a personal network and a professional network?

- Is it possible to translate my LinkedIn profile into multiple languages?
- What are the advantages of a Premium account?

If you use Facebook, Twitter or Instagram, you undoubtedly already have some skills that will help you on LinkedIn. However, LinkedIn is not like other social networks, and if you want to create an effective profile on the site, you will need to pay careful attention and have a clear idea of what you are looking for when you sign up.

LinkedIn, which is available in both free and Premium versions, allows users to build or strengthen a network of professional contacts, and to display their skills, education and work experience, making them more visible to recruiters.

> "When I joined LinkedIn, I opted for the Premium account, which is free for the first month, straight away. With a Premium account, you can add contacts even if you have no shared connections, send them messages and see who is looking at your profile. The Premium account unlocks a host of additional features, which makes it much more effective for job searching."

(Aurélie, Event Organiser)

However, LinkedIn is only effective if you maintain it by regularly adding new contacts in your sector, updating your profile and being active as often as possible in order to attract the attention of fellow professionals.

Whether you are looking for a new job, are trying to develop your network of professional contacts, or have a LinkedIn account but are unsure whether you are getting the best out of it, in under an hour this guide will talk you through the steps to follow in order to consolidate your professional relationships via LinkedIn.

LINKEDIN: THE BASICS

LinkedIn's stated aim is to "connect the world's professionals to make them more productive and successful". It is a sort of mini blog which allows you to showcase your skills, experiences, qualifications, network of contacts and achievements.

LinkedIn was launched in 2003 and now has over 530 million users worldwide (as of October 2017), making it a major international professional network. It enables users to develop their personal brand, network more effectively, promote their company and maximise their chances when job hunting. In professional terms, LinkedIn has become the place to be, both for recruiters and for jobseekers, as it provides each group with a range of tools.

OPTIMISING YOUR LINKEDIN PROFILE

A clear aim

Before you create or update your LinkedIn profile,

it is essential to take some time to think about what you want to achieve with it. For example, you could be looking for a new job, trying to develop your network or searching for talented new hires for a particular project. Your aim will determine what you include or emphasise in your profile. If you are looking for a job, you should focus on your skills, your areas of expertise and what you can offer a company. If you are trying to find people working in either the same sector as you or the sector you are interested in, you should highlight your contacts and achievements. You can order the headings however you want, which means that you can modify your profile based on your objectives.

Relevant information

If you want your LinkedIn profile to attract the attention of the right people, you need to be meticulous in filling it out (experience, qualifications, skills, region, summary, and so on), include as much detail as you can and be as precise as possible. Start with the most important information which is relevant to your aims, namely the sector you want to work in and the title of your current position (or the title of your profession, if you are currently out of work). This will allow anyone who visits your profile to identify your area of professional expertise immediately. Use relevant key words and try to be creative, as this will make you more likely to stand out. Make sure that you also include your contact information.

In the "Summary" section, write a brief description of yourself and your career so far, focusing on the most important information. In this section, it is best to write in the first person singular ("I") and use short sentences. What you are looking for right now should be immediately apparent, so you need to make sure that you update this section regularly. The "Summary" is the most read section of LinkedIn profiles, so it is vital that you pay close attention to it. Do not just copy and paste your CV: the idea is to pick out the best parts, summarise it and provide a short, engaging description of your professional experience and profile. Some users also outline their career objectives in this section. Whatever information you choose to emphasise, your summary should be concise: a few lines is the optimal length, so that recruiters can get a clear idea of your profile but do not have time to get distracted.

SOMETHING TO AVOID

If you want your LinkedIn profile to stand out, you need to choose your profile picture carefully. Avoid selfies, photos taken with your webcam, holiday photos, photos taken on a night out, blurry photos, and so on. Not including a photo is also a bad idea: profiles with a photograph are consulted far more frequently than anonymous profiles. You should therefore choose a recent profes-sional photo in which you look like yourself and are wearing work-appropriate clothing, without your partner, children or friends.

Do not neglect the multimedia dimension: add images and photographs with Pinterest or SlideShare, videos with YouTube or Vimeo, or sounds with SoundCloud or Mixcloud. You can also add documents and publications, such as your CV, cover letter, thesis, articles, books, and so on. You can add media to the "Introduction", "Experience" and "Education" sections, so make the most of the opportunity!

The "Skills" section, which allows you to list a series of skills based on terms used on the job market, also plays a vital role on LinkedIn. When you look for a skill, LinkedIn suggests a catalogue of the most frequently used terms and allows you to list up to 35. You can even add skills you have developed in your personal life, such as organising an annual dinner for your neighbourhood, writing if you have a blog, or any other skills that may be useful in your professional life. Include all the skills you believe you have in this section. Your colleagues, professors, employers, customers and interns can endorse you for these skills or write brief recommendations of your work which will be visible on your profile. The more relevant recommendations and endorsements you have, the more attention employers will pay to your profile.

BOOSTING YOUR VISIBILITY

The importance of your URL

LinkedIn allows all users to personalise their URL, which has two key benefits:

- You can share a professional-looking link to your profile. A clear, clean URL is much more appealing than a lengthy one featuring a string of meaningless numbers.
- Instead of your name, you can use your profes-

sion or role. This allows you to indicate your area of expertise directly or to give your profile a better chance of appearing in search engine results through the use of carefully chosen key words.

Once you have personalised your URL, you can add it to your email signature, your Facebook and Twitter pages, your CV, your business cards, and so on.

The impact of key words

To make your profile more visible and attract the attention of fellow professionals, you need to ensure that it has a good chance of appearing in search engine results. You can do this by incorporating key words throughout your profile, as recruiters find candidates to contact primarily by searching for key words in the "Skills", "Experience" and "Summary" sections. Make sure that you include these key words in your descriptions!

To work out which key words to use, put yourself in an employer's shoes and imagine that you are looking for a particular profile, or look at job postings to find the right terms. As a general rule, it is better to use action words or verbs rather than vague terms that describe your overall personality.

Carefully managed interactions

LinkedIn allows you to personalise your signature and incorporate it into your emails thanks to an HTML script. Several templates are available; all you have to do is fill in each field, making sure to include links to your profile, website or blog. Similarly, it may be worth adding a LinkedIn badge to your blog or website.

Using other social networks will enable you to further boost your profile's visibility. Add your websites, blogs, Twitter account and Facebook profile to your LinkedIn account. You can also directly connect your LinkedIn profile to your Twitter and Facebook pages through your account settings for the latter sites. This means that anything you publish on LinkedIn will appear on Twitter and Facebook (but not the other way around), which is a good way of making your friends aware of your LinkedIn profile and encouraging more people to visit it. However, if you do this you need to be extra careful about what you post and how often you post it, so that you do not overload any of your social networks with useless or irrelevant information.

LinkedIn allows you to link a range of other apps to your profile, such as your WordPress page. You can also use SlideShare, a LinkedIn product, to showcase your achievements. Other related sites include ProFinder, which helps you to find freelancers working in your area, and Marketing Solutions, which allows businesses to create their own advertisements and target their audience based on elements such as job title and sector.

MAKING NEW CONNECTIONS

Relationships on several levels

LinkedIn gives you a list of "People you may know", based on your studies, past experience and existing contacts. In order to connect with someone, you must have some link with them (university, workplace, internship, shared connections, and so on) and be able to prove this link. This prevents users from being inundated with spam requests. Your first step should therefore be to add the people you know through your education or professional experience by searching for your colleagues, former colleagues or acquaintances in your sector. The important thing is to fill your contacts list with people who match or complement your profile.

LinkedIn functions based on levels of relationships. The first level is your own connections, meaning the people with whom you are in direct contact through LinkedIn and who are part of your network. The second level refers to your contacts' contacts, while the third level comprises the contacts of the people on the second level. LinkedIn suggests people to add to your network based on these degrees of proximity, and allows Premium users to contact them directly via InMails, the site's direct messaging service.

When you send someone an invitation to connect, avoid the standard text offered by LinkedIn. Instead, personalise your message as much as possible, as it is this message that will make people decide whether or not to accept you. Remind the person who you are and how you met them, explain why you think your relationship will be useful and ask them to connect with you. Make sure you do not send too many invitations at once, as this may cause the site to erroneously identify you as a spammer.

A second- or third-degree connection can obviously contact you outside of LinkedIn if you have provided accurate contact details. If you can be contacted easily without going through a LinkedIn contact request (which means that users will not have to pay for an InMail), a lot more people will get in touch with you.

Group discussions

You can also expand your professional network on LinkedIn through groups. Taking part in specific groups and in these groups' discussions will allow you to get in contact with people in your sector. These groups bring together experts from the same field and make it possible to share advice and offer your opinion on a range of subjects. LinkedIn allows you to be a member of up to 100 groups. Being active in these groups is a good way of getting noticed by professionals in your sector and of expanding your network. However, make sure that you do not post too much and that your contributions remain relevant.

It can be useful to sort through the groups you belong to every so often. Since your professional interests are constantly changing, groups that were useful to you in the past may not be any more.

Maintain your network

Once you have built up your network, you need to maintain it by remaining active and paying attention to what your contacts are doing. If you see that somebody has got a new job, congratulate them. Do not ignore your contacts' questions if your experience allows you to provide a helpful response. Feel free to endorse your current or former colleagues, or to add a brief recommendation. The more you recommend your peers, the more likely they are to return the favour. The impact of this is twofold: on the one hand, it will highlight your skills and experiences, and, on the other hand, it will help you to maintain positive relationships with your contacts.

If you have a good relationship with particular colleagues or managers, do not hesitate to ask them to endorse you for some skills or to write you a recommendation, as endorsements and recommendations from people who work closely with you carry far more weight.

ADVICE FOR EMPLOYEES

Having a LinkedIn profile is not enough: if you remain passive and never update your profile, there is next to no chance of an employer coming across it. It is up to you to stay up to date with changes and job postings, and to react quickly to them. While you are waiting for your dream job to be posted, make your profile a source of quality content by posting news, information and advertisements. Get yourself noticed by interacting with other users, company pages or groups linked to your sector.

Premium accounts

If you feel that LinkedIn's standard features are not enough, you can access more by paying for a Premium account, which offers additional services and will help you make your profile more attractive. You have several different options, depending on your needs and objectives. If you are looking for a job, a Premium account will help you to get noticed by managers, get in touch with recruiters and send a message to any user without paying for an InMail, which will enable you to expand your network. LinkedIn Premium also makes life easier for employers, as it helps them to find people to hire more quickly. A Premium account also lets you see everyone who has viewed your profile.

SUMMARY

In order to optimise your LinkedIn profile, you need to:

- add an attention-grabbing title;
- make sure that it is complete and update it regularly;
- add photographs, videos, articles, docu-

ments and so on;
- incorporate targeted key words;
- join relevant groups and participate in some of their discussions;
- follow companies in your sector;
- build and maintain a network of contacts.

TOP TIPS

- **Consult the profiles of other LinkedIn users in your sector.** Make a note of everything that interests you and any details that recur across several profiles. This will help you to target the things that it is important to mention in order to make your profile effective.

- **Choose a suitable title.** The title of your profile appears just below your name and will show up in Google searches, so make sure it stands out!
- **Make it easier to contact you** by adding your email address, website, Facebook and Twitter profiles, etc. This will allow LinkedIn users who

are not connected to you to contact you easily if they come across your profile.

- **Go into detail**, especially in the "Experience" section, which allows you to add achievements and documents and to tag the companies you have worked for. Give as much detail as possible about your role and the projects you worked on.
- **Pay attention to multimedia.** Make the most of LinkedIn's features to add as much multi-media content as possible: hyperlinks, PDFs, PowerPoints, videos, images, photographs, and so on.

EXTRA INFORMATION

You can make your profile stand out and draw attention to it by posting updates about your work to it every day. This could include the projects you are currently working on (as long as they are not confidential, of course), a job posting at your company or relevant articles.

- **Be proactive.** Ask questions, take part in discussions in groups and sub-groups related to your profession, and give relevant responses to topical questions.
- **Feel free to create your own groups.** This will allow you to stand out from the crowd, showcase your skills, give and receive advice, and discuss topics related to your work.
- **Create alerts to get notifications about subjects you consider useful**, whether as part of your job search or your networking.
- **Endorse your connections' skills** – they are sure to return the favour! Your aim should be to acquire endorsements and recommendations from multiple people working in your sector throughout your career.

you based on your contacts. If they see that you have connections in your sector, they will pay more attention to your application. When you are trying to connect with people who you do not know personally, it is worth writing a personalised message.

- **Talk about yourself.** Feel free to add a few relevant personal details (for example about your passions, your hobbies, any humanitarian organisations or charities that you support, and so on). This will give recruiters a better idea of who you are as a person.
- **Keep your profile up to date.** For example, once you have built up more experience, consider deleting your internships, temporary roles or student jobs and leaving only your main experiences, the ones that are likely to have the most impact on your work in future.

Day-to-day maintenance

There are a number of actions you should carry out on LinkedIn on a day-to-day basis.

- Start by paying attention to your contacts:

endorse their skills, like their posts and congratulate them when they share important professional news.

- Next, focus on your profile: update information if you need to, share news, contribute to groups, look at who has viewed your profile, and search for and add new connections.
- Every now and then, sort through your contacts, groups, experience, etc.

FAQS

SHOULD LINKEDIN BE USED TO COMPLEMENT OTHER SOCIAL NETWORKS?

LinkedIn is a professional network. It should therefore be kept separate from other, more informal social networks such as Facebook, Twitter, Instagram and Pinterest, and can be used in parallel to them.

In order to make your profile on a professional network effective, you need to devote some time to it every day and regularly set aside slots in your timetable to update it. It is best to focus your attentions on a single professional network so that you can make the most of its features, and to use other social networks for different, more personal reasons. There is no need to use every social network to showcase your professional accomplishments. That said, sites such as Facebook can still be used for professional purposes.

SHOULD I PUBLISH PERSONAL INFORMATION ON LINKEDIN?

As is the case with a CV, some aspects of your personality are worth highlighting to improve your professional image (for example, if you volunteer or support a humanitarian cause). Recruiters care about how you spend your free time and what you are like as a person, since you may end up working with them. Including some flattering personal details is therefore a good strategy to reassure recruiters. However, do not reveal too much, and keep some aspects of your personal life private (your family situation, for example).

When you are looking for a new job but are still with your current company, it is better if your employer does not see your LinkedIn profile. You can adjust your privacy settings by clicking on the drop-down menu marked "Me" in the top right-hand corner in order to prevent your colleagues from receiving notifications about changes to your profile, new contacts and new groups that you have joined. In short, your privacy settings will allow you to hide the fact that you are looking for new opportunities from your current employer.

SHOULD I LIST ALL MY PROFESSIONAL EXPERIENCE ON MY PROFILE?

LinkedIn is a tool that allows you to sell yourself, no matter what "buyer" you are looking for (business partner, employer, etc.). It is better to select the most relevant experiences that are linked to your career path rather than indiscriminately adding all your work experience, including internships and student jobs. Choose a few roles and specify the skills you acquired and your main accomplishments in a few concise sentences. Go into detail without being wordy. Tailor your profile as closely as possible to your goals by including only the most relevant parts of your education and training and the most relevant roles you have occupied. Having said that, make sure that you do not leave long periods of time unaccounted for, as this will make it seem as though you have not been working.

EXTRA INFORMATION

To complete your profile, do not forget to put links to your website, blog, professional Facebook page, YouTube page (if you work in the audiovisual sector, for example), and so on, in the introduction section where they will be more visible. This will direct users to other pages showcasing your skills and accomplishments.

SHOULD I MAKE MY LINKEDIN PROFILE PUBLIC?

Like with all social networks, you can adjust your privacy settings on LinkedIn. Specifically, you can choose who can view your activity and updates, and what people who are not connected to you can see when they consult your profile. It is up to you to decide what information you make public. Ideally, you should avoid revealing too much at the outset, as keeping some information hidden will encourage professionals to add you to their network of contacts if they want to know more. You can expand your network by awakening people's curiosity.

IS THERE A DIFFERENCE BETWEEN A PERSONAL NETWORK AND A PROFESSIONAL NETWORK?

We strongly recommend keeping your personal and professional lives separate. This is parti-cularly true on social networks, and especially on professional networks. Stick to Facebook, Twitter and Instagram for personal use but, as we have already said, this does not mean that you cannot use your personal networks to exchange professional information in some situations.

IS IT POSSIBLE TO TRANSLATE MY LINKEDIN PROFILE INTO MULTIPLE LANGUAGES?

You can publish your profile in several languages, which is a useful option if you are considering working abroad as it increases your visibility for recruiters who are based in other countries or whose first language is not English.

WHAT ARE THE ADVANTAGES OF A PREMIUM ACCOUNT?

The Premium account costs money and allows you to use other LinkedIn features and optimise your profile. There are four versions of the Premium account (Career, Business, Sales and Hiring), which each have different features but have some shared advantages to help you to find your dream job, contact whoever you want, find talent and increase your commercial opportunities. With a Premium account, you can also see the complete list of people who have consulted your profile. Finally, the Open Profile option means that anyone can see your full profile and get in touch with you.

OVER TO YOU

PROFILE CHECKLIST

To optimise your profile and make sure that you have not forgotten anything, use the checklist below to create and update it.

	Check
Profile	
Photograph	
Title	
Summary	
Education	
Skills	
Experience	
URL	
Contacts	
Searching on multiple levels	
Sending requests (automatic or personalised)	
Interactions (congratulations, questions and answers, and so on)	
Recommendations	

	Check
Groups	
Signing up	
Interaction (questions and answers, advice, and so on)	
Other	
Key words	
Multimedia (photographs, videos, SlideShare, and so on)	
Links to other social networks or websites	
Apps	

We want to hear from you!
Leave a comment on your online library
and share your favourite books on social media!

FURTHER READING

BIBLIOGRAPHY

- Comment ça marche. (2017) *Optimiser son profil LinkedIn et développer son réseau.* [Online]. [Accessed 23 October 2017]. Available from: <http://www.commentcamarche.net/faq/32052-optimiser-son-profil-linkedin-et-developper-son-reseau>

- Guicharnaud, A. (2015) 5 points à changer immédiatement sur votre profil LinkedIn. *L'Obs.* [Online]. [Accessed 23 October 2017]. Available from: <http://tempsreel.nouvelobs.com/bien-bien/20150618.OBS1104/5-points-a-changer-immediatement-sur-votre-profil-linkedin.html>

- Huffington Post. (2013) *Les 8 erreurs à ne jamais commettre sur LinkedIn.* [Online]. [Accessed 23 October 2017]. Available from: <http://www.huffingtonpost.fr/learnvest/erreurs-profil-linkedin_b_2866683.html>

- Lareng, J-P. (2014) *Les 7 points clé d'un profil LinkedIn attractif.* [Online]. [Accessed 23 October 2017]. Available from: <https://www.linkedin.com/pulse/20140713130047-36412962-les-7-points-cl%C3%A9-d-un-profil-linkedin-attractif/>

- Lhameen, S. (2013) LinkedIn : 6 conseils pour créer

votre profil parfait. *Cadre Dirigeant Magazine.* [Online]. [Accessed 23 October 2017]. Available from: <http://www.cadre-dirigeant-magazine. com/reussir-en-entreprise/vie-quotidien-cadre/ linkedin-6-conseils-creer-profil-parfait/>

- LinkedIn. (No date) *About Us.* [Online]. [Accessed 23 October 2017]. Available from: <https://press. linkedin.com/about-linkedin>

- March, V. (2015) *Comment développer votre activité grâce aux médias sociaux.* Malakoff: Dunod.

- Payet, G. (2015) *5 conseils pour améliorer votre profil LinkedIn.* [Online]. [Accessed 23 October 2017]. Available from: <http://www.20minutes. fr/economie/1614299-20150526-5-conseils -ameliorer-profil-linkedin>

- Robveille, J. (2012) Rendre votre profil LinkedIn irrésistible en 11 étapes. *Social Media For You.* [Online]. [Accessed 23 October 2017]. Available from: <https://www.social-media-for-you. com/11-astuces-pour-rendre-votre-profil-linke- din-irresistible/>

- Ropars, F. (2015) 10 conseils pour optimiser son profil LinkedIn. *Blog du Moderateur.* [Online]. [Accessed 23 October 2017]. Available from: <https://www.blogdumoderateur.com/ optimiser-profil-linkedin/>

- Werth, H. (No date) LinkedIn : le guide pour un profil complet et plus visible sur LinkedIn. *LinkedIn.* [Online]. [Accessed 23 October 2017]. Available

from: <https://business.linkedin.com/content/
dam/business/talent-solutions/regional/fr_FR/
site/pdf/playbooks/linkedin-guide-profil-complet.
pdf>

ADDITIONAL SOURCES

- Evrard, J. (2017) *Networking*. Trans. Foster, J.
  Brussels: Plurilingua Publishing.

- Spies, N. (2017) *Job Seeking on Social Media*. Trans.
  Neal, R. Brussels: Plurilingua Publishing.

IMPROVE YOUR GENERAL KNOWLEDGE

IN A BLINK OF AN EYE !

www.50minutes.com